Congressional
Research Service
Informing the legislative debate since 1914

Organization of American States: Background and Issues for Congress

Peter J. Meyer
Analyst in Latin American Affairs

August 29, 2014

Congressional Research Service

7-5700

www.crs.gov

R42639

Summary

Contents

Tables

Contacts

Introduction

Over the past several years, there has been considerable congressional debate over the role of the Organization of American States (OAS) in the Western Hemisphere and its utility for advancing U.S. objectives in the region. The United States helped found the OAS in 1948 in order to establish a multilateral forum in which the nations of the hemisphere could engage one another and address issues of mutual concern. In subsequent decades, OAS decisions often reflected U.S. policy as other member states sought to maintain close relations with the dominant economic and political power in the hemisphere. This was especially true during the early Cold War period, when the United States was able to secure OAS support for initiatives that were controversial in the region, such as a 1962 resolution to exclude Cuba from active participation as a result of its adherence to Marxism-Leninism and association with the communist bloc. OAS actions again aligned closely with U.S. policy in the 1990s following the end of the Cold War as a result of strong consensus among member states in support of initiatives designed to liberalize markets and strengthen democratic governance.[1]

According to many foreign policy analysts,[2] the ability of the United States to exert authority and shape outcomes in the Western Hemisphere—a region critical to U.S. political, economic, and security interests—has declined over the past decade. This is the result of a number of trends. Citizens throughout Latin America and the Caribbean have elected ideologically diverse leaders, bringing an end to the post-Cold War policy consensus. At the same time, many countries in the region have enjoyed considerable economic growth, grown more confident in addressing their own challenges, and diversified their commercial and diplomatic relations. These developments have enabled countries in the region to pursue more independent foreign policies that are less deferential to the United States.[3] The relative decline of U.S. influence in the Western Hemisphere has manifested itself within the OAS on a number of high profile decisions in recent years, including a 2009 decision to repeal the 1962 resolution that had suspended Cuba from participating in the organization.[4]

---

[1] George Meek, "U.S. Influence in the Organization of American States," *Journal of Interamerican Studies and World Affairs*, vol. 17, no. 3 (August 1975), pp. 311-325; Carolyn M. Shaw, "Limits to Hegemonic Influence in the Organization of American States," *Latin American Politics and Society*, vol. 45, no. 3 (Autumn 2003), pp. 59-92; Pedro Ernesto Fagundes, "A Atuação da Organização dos Estados Americanos (OEA) nas Crises Políticas Contemporâneas," *Meridiano*, vol. 47, no. 117 (April 2010), pp. 30-32.

[2] See, for example, Inter-American Dialogue, *Remaking the Relationship: The United States and Latin America*, April 2012; Russell Crandall, "The Post-American Hemisphere: Power and Politics in an Autonomous Latin America," *Foreign Affairs*, vol. 90, no. 3 (May/June 2011), pp. 83-95; and Council on Foreign Relations, *U.S. Latin America Relations: A New Direction for a New Reality*, Independent Task Force Report No. 60, New York, 2008.

[3] Michael Shifter, "Managing Disarray: The Search for a New Consensus," in *Which Way Latin America? Hemispheric Politics Meets Globalization*, eds. Andrew F. Cooper and Jorge Heine (United Nations University Press, 2009); Brookings Institution, *Rethinking U.S.-Latin American Relations: A Hemispheric Partnership for a Turbulent World*, Report of the Partnership for the Americas Commission, Washington, DC, November 2008; and Peter Hakim, "The United States and Latin America: The Neighborhood has Changed," *International Spectator*, vol. 46, no. 4 (December 2011), pp. 63-78.

[4] Mike Leffert, "Organization of American States Reinstates Cuba by Consensus Despite U.S. Objections," *Latin America Data Base, NotiCen*, June 4, 2009. For more information, see "Reintegration of Cuba into the Inter-American System" below.

U.S. policy makers have responded to the United States' declining ability to advance its policy preferences within the OAS in a number of ways. Some Members of Congress have alleged that the OAS has allied itself with anti-U.S. regimes, and is weakening democracy in Latin America. Accordingly, they have argued that support for the OAS runs counter to U.S. objectives in the hemisphere, and that the United States should withhold funding from the organization. Others have disagreed, arguing that OAS actions continue to closely align with U.S. priorities in many cases, and that defunding the OAS would amount to the United States turning its back on the Western Hemisphere. They have asserted that weakening the one multilateral forum that includes every democratic nation of the hemisphere would strengthen the hands of hostile governments while further weakening U.S. influence in the region.[5]

As Congress continues to debate the utility of the OAS for advancing U.S. policies and considers appropriations and other legislation related to the organization, it might examine OAS activities in the hemisphere and how well those activities align with U.S. objectives. This report briefly looks at the history of the OAS and its principal institutional bodies; examines the organization's funding and current priorities; and discusses a number of policy issues that have drawn congressional interest in recent years, including the reintegration of Cuba into the inter-American system, application of the Inter-American Democratic Charter, potential reforms of the inter-American human rights system, the management and budget of the OAS, and the establishment of regional organizations that could serve as possible alternatives to the OAS.

Background

History and Purpose

The OAS charter was adopted on April 30, 1948, in Bogotá, Colombia, though multilateral relations among the countries of the Western Hemisphere go back much further. A series of inter-American conferences that began in the 1820s led to the creation of the International Union of American Republics in 1890. Originally created to collect and distribute commercial information, the International Union of American Republics was renamed the Pan American Union in 1910. In 1933, following the launch of President Franklin Roosevelt's "Good Neighbor" policy, the United States and other nations in the hemisphere signed the Convention on the Rights and Duties of States, which formally recognized the equality of states and the principle of nonintervention in one another's internal affairs. Close cooperation during World War II considerably strengthened hemispheric ties, which were reinforced in the post-war period with the adoption of the Inter-American Treaty of Reciprocal Assistance (Rio Treaty) in 1947. The OAS Charter and American Declaration of the Rights and Duties of Man were signed a year later by the United States and 20 other countries[6] in the region to legally codify the institutions and principles that had come to form the inter-American system.

---

[5] Josh Rogin, "House Panel Votes to Defund the OAS," *Foreign Policy: The Cable*, July 20, 2011; U.S. Congress, House Committee on Foreign Affairs, Subcommittee on the Western Hemisphere, *Markup on H.R. 3401 and H.R. 2542*, Hearing, 112th Cong., 1st sess., December 15, 2011, Serial No. 112-115 (Washington: GPO, 2011), http://foreignaffairs.house.gov/112/72103.pdf; and "Dissenting Views" in H.Rept. 112-223.

[6] The OAS has expanded over time. All 35 independent nations in the hemisphere have now signed the charter.

Although the OAS initially sought to address border disputes and collective security issues, it has expanded its activities into other areas over time. In 1959, the Inter-American Commission on Human Rights was created to carry out the provisions of the American Declaration of the Rights and Duties of Man. During the 1960s, the OAS greatly expanded its economic, social, cultural, scientific, and technological programs, placing a strong emphasis on development following the 1961 launch of President Kennedy's "Alliance for Progress." Abuses by authoritarian governments prompted the creation of the Inter-American Court of Human Rights in 1978, and growing concern over narcotics trafficking led to the establishment of the Inter-American Drug Abuse Control Commission in 1986. The OAS acknowledged the challenges posed by regional and international terrorism by creating the Inter-American Committee Against Terrorism in 1999, and recognized the near universal commitment to democracy in the region through the adoption of the Inter-American Democratic Charter in 2001.[7]

According to the OAS Charter, as amended, the purpose of the organization is to:

- strengthen the peace and security of the continent;

- promote and consolidate representative democracy, with due respect for the principle of nonintervention;

- prevent possible causes of difficulties and ensure the pacific settlement of disputes that may arise among member states;

- provide for common action on the part of those states in the event of aggression;

- seek the solution of political, juridical, and economic problems that may arise among them;

- promote, by cooperative action, their economic, social, and cultural development;

- eradicate extreme poverty, which constitutes an obstacle to the full democratic development of the peoples of the hemisphere; and

- achieve an effective limitation of conventional weapons that will make it possible to devote the largest amount of resources to the economic and social development of member states.[8]

Institutional Bodies

The OAS is composed of a variety of councils, committees, and other institutional organs, some of which are autonomous. There are three primary bodies, however, that are responsible for setting and carrying out the agenda of the OAS: the General Assembly, the Permanent Council, and the General Secretariat.

---

[7] U.S. Congress, Senate Committee on Foreign Relations and House Committee on Foreign Affairs, *Inter-American Relations: A Collection of Documents, Legislation, Descriptions of Inter-American Organizations, and Other Material Pertaining to Inter-American Affairs*, Joint Committee Print, Prepared by the Congressional Research Service, 100th Cong., 2nd sess., December 1988, S.Prt. 100-168 (Washington: GPO, 1989); O. Carlos Stoetzer, *The Organization of American States*, 2nd ed. (Westport, CT: Praeger, 1993); and OAS, "Our History," http://www.oas.org/en/about/our_history.asp.

[8] OAS, *Charter of the Organization of American States*, http://www.oas.org/juridico/english/charter html.

General Assembly

The General Assembly is the principal policy-making organ of the OAS. It meets annually[9] to debate current issues, approve the organization's budget, and set policies to govern the other OAS bodies. The General Assembly is composed of the delegations of each of the 34 participating member states,[10] with each state having a single vote. It is empowered to adopt most decisions with the affirmative votes of an absolute majority of the member states; however, some decisions, including the adoption of the agenda and the approval of budgetary matters, require the affirmative votes of two-thirds of the member states. In practice, the General Assembly tends to operate by consensus. The most recent General Assembly was held in Asunción Paraguay on June 3-5, 2014, and focused on "Development with Social Inclusion."

Permanent Council

The day-to-day business of the OAS is conducted by the Permanent Council, which meets regularly throughout the year at the organization's headquarters in Washington, DC. Among other activities, the Permanent Council works to maintain friendly relations among member states, assists in the peaceful settlement of disputes, carries out decisions assigned to it by the General Assembly, regulates the General Secretariat when the General Assembly is not in session, receives reports from the various bodies of the inter-American system, and submits recommendations to the General Assembly. Additionally, the Permanent Council is empowered by the Inter-American Democratic Charter to undertake necessary diplomatic initiatives in the event of an unconstitutional alteration of government. Each member state appoints one representative to the Permanent Council, and each member state has a single vote. The affirmative votes of two-thirds of the member states are required for most Permanent Council decisions. Like the General Assembly, however, the Permanent Council tends to operate by consensus.

General Secretariat

The General Secretariat, directed by the Secretary General and the Assistant Secretary General, is the permanent body charged with implementing the policies set by the General Assembly and the Permanent Council. The Secretary General and the Assistant Secretary General are elected by the General Assembly and serve five-year terms with the possibility of one re-election. According to the OAS Charter, the Secretary General serves as the legal representative of the organization and is allowed to participate in all OAS meetings with a voice but without a vote. The Secretary General is also empowered to establish offices and hire personnel to implement OAS mandates. Some analysts maintain that—given the virtual paralysis of the organization that can result from differences among member states and the need for consensus—"the effectiveness of the OAS critically depends on the consistent, vigorous, and sometimes risk-taking leadership of the Secretary General."[11]

---

[9] A special session of the General Assembly can be convoked by a two-thirds vote of the Permanent Council.

[10] Although the OAS technically has 35 member states, Cuba does not currently participate in the OAS. See "Reintegration of Cuba into the Inter-American System" below for more information.

[11] Inter-American Dialogue, *Responding to the Hemisphere's Political Challenges: Report of the Inter-American Dialogue Task Force on the Organization of American States*, June 2006, p. 7.

The current Secretary General is José Miguel Insulza of Chile. He was first elected in 2005, and was reelected in 2010. Insulza's term is scheduled to end in May 2015. Candidates to succeed him as Secretary General include Uruguayan Foreign Minister Luis Almagro, former Guatemalan Vice President Eduardo Stein, and Diego García Sayán, a Peruvian currently serving as a judge on the Inter-American Court of Human Rights.

Budget

The OAS budget is expected to total $167 million in 2014 (see **Table 1**). The largest portion of the budget is the Regular Fund, which primarily supports the operations of the General Secretariat. The Regular Fund is principally financed through the assessed contributions, or membership dues, of OAS member states. Assessed contributions are calculated based on gross national income, with adjustments for debt burden and low per capita income.[12] Since 1997, the OAS has sought to supplement the Regular Fund by collecting Specific Funds—voluntary contributions from member states and other international donors that are directed to specific projects or programs. Although Specific Funds contributions now account for roughly half of the total OAS budget, the organization has faced persistent budget shortfalls for a number of years (for more information, see "Management and Budget Concerns" below).

Table 1. Organization of American States Budget: 2010-2014

(Millions of current U.S. dollars)

	2010	2011	2012	2013	2014
Regular Fund	90.1	83.0	83.5	83.9	83.0
Specific Funds	74.6	77.9	63.1	72.0	78.8
Indirect Cost Recovery (ICR)ᵃ	6.4	7.7	5.2	5.3	5.3
Total	171.1	168.6	151.8	161.1	167.0

Source: OAS, Office of the Secretary General, *Program-Budgets of the Organization, 2013-2014.*

a. A certain percentage (usually 11-12%) of each contribution to a Specific Fund is transferred to the ICR account to defray indirect costs incurred by the General Secretariat in administering Specific Fund activities.

The United States is the top source of funding for the OAS. It contributed at least $65.7 million in FY2013—equivalent to 41% of the total 2013 OAS budget (see **Table 2**). In 2013, the largest member state donors after the United States were Canada ($22.6 million), Brazil ($8.7 million), Mexico ($7.9 million), Colombia ($3.5 million), and Argentina ($2.6 million). The largest nonmember donors were the Netherlands ($8.8 million), the European Union ($3.1 million), Sweden ($1.1 million), Switzerland ($902,000), and Germany ($733,000).[13]

---

[12] Currently, the maximum contribution any nation could be assessed against the budget is 59.47% and the minimum is 0.022%. OAS, Office of the Secretary General, *Proposed Program-Budget, 2014*, August 5, 2013.

[13] OAS, *4ᵗʰ Quarterly Resource Management and Performance Report, January 1 to December 31, 2013*, February 20, 2014. Non-hemispheric nations can be granted "permanent observer status" which permits them to participate in OAS activities and contribute to OAS programs. Currently, there are 70 "permanent observer" nations.

Table 2. U.S. Funding for the OAS: FY2010-FY2015

(Millions of current U.S. dollars)

	FY2010	FY2011	FY2012	FY2013	FY2014 (est.)	FY2015 (req.)
Regular Fund	47.1	48.1	48.5	48.5	48.5	48.5
Specific Funds	17.6	13.3	17.9	17.2	7.9	6.1
[Development Fund]	[5.0]	[4.8]	[3.5]	[3.3]	[3.4]	[3.4]
[Democracy Fund]	[3.0]	[3.0]	[4.5]	[4.3]	[4.5]	[2.7]
[Other]ª	[9.6]	[5.5]	[9.9]	[9.6]	[na]	[na]
Total	64.7	61.4	67.5	65.7	56.4	54.6
% of OAS Budgetᵇ	37.8	36.4	44.5	40.8	33.8	na

Source: U.S. Department of State, *Congressional Budget Justifications for FY2012-FY2015*; Explanatory Statement accompanying the Consolidated Appropriations Act, 2014 (P.L. 113-76); and data provided to CRS by the U.S. Mission to the OAS in February 2012, February 2013, and January 2014.

Notes: U.S. contributions to the Regular Fund are provided through the Contributions to International Organizations (CIO) account, and voluntary contributions for the OAS Development and Democracy Funds are provided through the International Organization and Programs (IO&P) account.

a. Some U.S. agencies may have provided additional contributions to the OAS beyond those captured here. Since these voluntary contributions are not included in the annual budget request and are provided over the course of each fiscal year, it is not yet known what total U.S. funding will be in FY2014 or FY2015.

b. Calculated using total U.S. contributions per fiscal year as a percentage of the annual OAS budget. The OAS sets its budget by calendar years.

The United States is currently responsible for providing 59.47% of the organization's assessed dues. In FY2014, the U.S. assessed contribution is expected to total $48.5 million. A provision of the OAS Revitalization and Reform Act of 2013 (P.L. 113-41), signed into law on October 2, 2013, calls on the OAS to alter its fee structure within five years so that no member state is responsible for more than 50% of the organization's assessed dues.

In addition to the assessed contribution, the United States is providing at least $7.9 million in voluntary contributions to the OAS in FY2013. Most U.S. voluntary contributions are provided through the OAS Development Assistance Fund (hereinafter Development Fund) and the OAS Fund for Strengthening Democracy (hereinafter Democracy Fund). Much of the financial support for the Development Fund is directed to the Special Multilateral Fund of the Inter-American Council for Integral Development (FEMCIDI), which finances national and multinational development projects. Other funding supports U.S. strategic goals at the Summits of the Americas[14] and projects such as the Inter-American Social Protection Network and the Energy and Climate Partnership of the Americas. The Democracy Fund provides assistance for a number

---

[14] The Summits of the Americas are institutionalized gatherings where the heads of state and government of the Western Hemisphere meet and discuss how to address common challenges. They have taken place every three to four years since 1994. The Sixth Summit of the Americas was held in Cartagena, Colombia in April 2012. The OAS serves as the technical secretariat for the Summits of the Americas, and is responsible for carrying out some of the mandates issued by the member states.

of activities in the region, including electoral observation missions, the Inter-American Commission on Human Rights, and technical assistance for member state electoral bodies.

While U.S. contributions to the Development and Democracy Funds are included in annual appropriations requests, various U.S. agencies generally provide additional voluntary contributions to other OAS programs over the course of each fiscal year. In recent years, these additional contributions have supported programs such as the Inter-American Drug Abuse Commission, the Inter-American Committee against Terrorism, and the Follow-Up Mechanism on Implementation of the Inter-American Convention against Corruption. According to the U.S. Mission to the OAS, U.S. voluntary contributions provide the United States with leverage to support initiatives that advance U.S. strategic goals and interests in the organization and region.[15]

The Obama Administration has requested $54.6 million for contributions to the OAS in FY2015. This includes $48.5 million for the assessed contribution and $6.1 million for voluntary contributions. The actual amount that will be provided to the OAS is currently unclear. According to the report (S.Rept. 113-195) accompanying the FY2015 Department of State, Foreign Operations, and Related Programs Appropriations Act (S. 2499), the bill would reduce funding for the U.S. assessed contribution to the OAS by 5%. It would also provide $9.5 million in voluntary contributions, including $3 million for the Development Fund, $4.5 million for the Democracy Fund, and $2 million for the Inter-American Commission on Human Rights. The House Appropriations Committee's version of the bill (H.R. 5013) and its accompanying report (H.Rept. 113-499) do not designate specific funding levels for the OAS.

Current Priorities

Upon taking office in May 2005, Secretary General Insulza identified democracy, human rights, integral development, and multidimensional security as the "fundamental pillars of the OAS."[16] He has reaffirmed his commitment to those pillars since winning reelection in 2010, asserting that his second term priorities include:

- strengthening democratic governance by promoting respect for the rule of law and institutions, independent and effective justice systems, full freedom of expression for all citizens, and transparency and accountability by public officials;

- enhancing the human rights system by promoting respect for and compliance with its decisions, ratification of the American Convention of Human Rights by all countries, and the continued struggle against all forms of discrimination;

- striking a better balance between democracy-building and integral development efforts by focusing activities on the mandates of the Summits of the Americas with respect to poverty and decent work, migration, competitiveness, energy, the environment and climate change, technological development, and education; and

---

[15] U.S. Mission to the OAS, "OAS Programs and Initiatives Receiving Direct USG/USOAS Funding," provided to CRS in February 2012.

[16] OAS document, CP/doc. 4071/05, *Meeting the Political Priorities of the Organization of American States*, December 14, 2005, p. 1.

- contributing to the enhancement of multidimensional security in the Americas by focusing efforts on the serious public security crisis generated by trafficking in drugs, arms, and persons; money laundering; and organized crime.[17]

These priorities are relatively consistent with the Obama Administration's policy toward the region, which is designed to strengthen effective democratic institutions, promote economic and social opportunity, secure a clean energy future, and ensure citizen security.[18]

Democracy Promotion

The OAS has taken a much more active role in promoting and defending democracy since the end of the Cold War and the return to civilian governance in most of the hemisphere. Member states approved a series of instruments designed to support democratic governance,[19] culminating in the adoption of the Inter-American Democratic Charter on September 11, 2001. The charter asserts that the peoples of the Americas have a right to democracy and their governments have an obligation to promote and defend it.[20] The OAS has sought to uphold these commitments through a number of activities, which include support for, and observation of, elections; technical assistance and other programs to foster institutional development and good governance; and the coordination of collective action when democratic institutions are threatened. While many analysts assert that the OAS has played an important role in normalizing democratic governance in the region,[21] some scholars maintain that the organization is selective in its defense of democracy.[22]

Electoral Observation Missions

One of the primary ways in which the OAS promotes democracy is through electoral observation missions. Since its first observation mission in 1962, the OAS has observed more than 200 electoral processes in 27 countries in the hemisphere.[23] Over the years, the OAS has earned a reputation for impartiality and technical competence, playing an important role in the legitimization of electoral processes as many Latin American and Caribbean countries

---

[17] Secretary General José Miguel Insulza, "Remarks by Secretary General of the OAS, Inaugural Ceremony Fortieth Regular Session of the General Assembly," June 6, 2010.

[18] For more information on U.S. policy and interests in the hemisphere, see CRS Report R42956, *Latin America and the Caribbean: Key Issues for the 113th Congress*, coordinated by Mark P. Sullivan.

[19] In 1991, the OAS General Assembly adopted resolution 1080, which instructs the Secretary General to convoke the Permanent Council or the General Assembly in the event of an interruption of democratic governance in a member state. The following year, the OAS became the first regional political organization to allow the suspension of a member state for the forceful overthrow of a democratically constituted government when it ratified an amendment to its charter known as the Washington Protocol.

[20] OAS, *Inter-American Democratic Charter*, http://www.oas.org/OASpage/eng/Documents/Democractic_Charter htm.

[21] See, for example, Canadian Foundation for the Americas (FOCAL), "Election Monitoring in the Americas," *FOCALPoint*, vol. 9, no. 1 (February 2010); and Pablo Policzer, *The Next Stage of Democracy Promotion*, FOCAL, Note Politique, July 2010.

[22] See, for example, Craig Arceneaux and David Pinion-Berlin, "Issues, Threats, and Institutions: Explaining OAS Responses to Democratic Dilemmas in Latin America," *Latin American Politics and Society*, vol. 49, no. 2 (2007), pp. 1-31; and Barry S. Levitt, "A Desultory Defense of Democracy: OAS Resolution 1080 and the Inter-American Democratic Charter," *Latin American Politics and Society*, vol. 48, no.3 (2006), pp. 93-123.

[23] OAS, "Secretary General Insulza Welcomes 'OAS Electoral Observation Day'," Press Release, February 4, 2013.

---

transitioned from authoritarian rule to representative democracy.[24] Some analysts have been critical of OAS observation missions in certain instances, however, maintaining that the organization has occasionally offered legitimacy to flawed elections.[25]

Today, the objectives of OAS electoral observation missions include observing electoral processes; encouraging citizen participation; verifying compliance with election laws; ensuring electoral processes are conducted in impartial, reliable, and transparent manners; and making recommendations to improve electoral systems. The OAS observes several electoral processes every year, but each mission must be invited by the country holding the election and must solicit separate funding from the international donor community. To date in 2014, the OAS has monitored six electoral processes in five countries: Antigua and Barbuda, Colombia, Costa Rica, El Salvador, and Panama.[26]

Institutional Strengthening

The OAS also promotes democracy by providing technical assistance to member states designed to strengthen institutions and improve good governance. Among other activities, the organization's Secretariat for Political Affairs conducts research, provides training in public management, analyzes risk factors for democratic instability, and promotes cooperation among government officials. It also supports conflict resolution efforts. The OAS Mission to Support the Peace Process in Colombia, for example, provides verification and advisory support to the Colombian government regarding the demobilization and reintegration into society of illegal armed groups.[27]

In 1996, OAS member states adopted the Inter-American Convention Against Corruption.[28] The convention is designed to improve government transparency by strengthening anti-corruption laws and facilitating cooperation among member states. Under the follow-up mechanism on the implementation of the convention, member states submit themselves to a reciprocal review process that evaluates how well they are implementing the convention, formulates recommendations for improving anti-corruption efforts, and facilitates the exchange of information to harmonize the region's anti-corruption legal frameworks.[29]

Collective Defense of Democracy

In addition to supporting elections and institutional strengthening activities, the OAS undertakes diplomatic initiatives designed to protect and restore democracy. As noted previously, by adopting

---

[24] U.S. Permanent Mission to the OAS, "Democracy Promotion & Human Rights," http://www.usoas.usmission.gov/democracy.html.

[25] See, for example, David Rosnick, *The Organization of American States in Haiti: Election Monitoring or Political Intervention?*, Center for Economic and Policy Research (CEPR), Washington, DC, August 2011; and Rubén M. Perina, "The Future of Electoral Observation," *Americas Quarterly*, (Spring 2012).

[26] OAS, "Electoral Observation Section," http://www.oas.org/es/sap/deco/moe.asp.

[27] OAS, "Secretariat for Political Affairs," http://www.oas.org/en/spa/default.asp; U.S. Permanent Mission to the OAS, "Democracy Promotion & Human Rights," http://www.usoas.usmission.gov/democracy.html.

[28] President Clinton submitted the Inter-American Convention Against Corruption to the Senate, for its advice and consent, in April 1998 (Treaty Doc. 105-39), and the Senate agreed to the resolution in July 2000. The text of the treaty is available at http://www.oas.org/juridico/english/treaties/b-58 html.

[29] OAS, "Anti-Corruption Portal of the Americas," http://www.oas.org/juridico/english/FightCur html.

the Inter-American Democratic Charter, OAS member states accepted an obligation to promote and defend democratic governance. However, disagreements among member states regarding when it is appropriate for the OAS to apply the provisions of the Democratic Charter have limited the organization's actions. Article 20 of the Democratic Charter—which allows for collective action "in the event of an unconstitutional alteration of the constitutional regime that seriously impairs the democratic order in a member state"—has been invoked by the OAS on only three occasions, each of which followed the ouster of a President.[30] In other instances, such as conflicts between branches of government or the erosion of liberal democratic institutions by democratically elected leaders, member states generally have been unwilling to support bold OAS actions, deferring instead to the principle of nonintervention.[31] (For more discussion of the charter and its application, see "Application of the Inter-American Democratic Charter" below).

Human Rights Protection

Many analysts consider the inter-American human rights system to be the most effective part of the OAS.[32] Unlike most of the organization's bodies, the Inter-American Commission on Human Rights (IACHR) and the Inter-American Court of Human Rights are autonomous, allowing them to execute their mandates to promote and protect human rights[33] without needing to establish consensus among member states on every action. Consequently, advocates maintain, the two bodies are able to take on the "pivotal role of condemnation and early warning in response to situations that undermine the consolidation of democracy and rule of law" in the hemisphere.[34]

In the first decades after its 1959 inception, the IACHR's documentation of human rights violations brought international attention to the abuses of repressive regimes. Although the human rights situation in the hemisphere has improved significantly as countries have transitioned away from dictatorships to democratic governments, the IACHR continues to play a significant role. Among other actions, the IACHR receives, analyzes, and investigates individual petitions alleging human rights violations. In recent years, it has received roughly 1,500 such petitions annually.[35] It also issues requests to governments to adopt "precautionary measures" in certain cases where individuals or groups are at risk of suffering serious and irreparable harm to their human rights. The IACHR receives several hundred petitions for precautionary measures

---

[30] Article 20 of the Democratic Charter was invoked after President Hugo Chávez was temporarily removed from power in Venezuela in 2002, several months after Haitian President Jean-Bertrand Aristide went into exile in 2004, and following the ouster of President Manuel Zelaya in Honduras in 2009. See: OAS documents, AG/RES. 1 (XXIX-E/02), *Support for Democracy in Venezuela*, April 18, 2002; AG/RES. 2058 (XXXIV-O/04), *Situation in Haiti: Strengthening of Democracy*, June 8, 2004; and AG/RES.1 (XXXVII-E/09), *Resolution on the Political Crisis in Honduras*, July 1, 2009.

[31] Arceneaux and Pinion-Berlin, 2007, op. cit.

[32] See, for example, Victoria Amato, "Taking Stock of the Reflection on the Workings of the Inter-American Commission on Human Rights," *Aportes: Magazine of the Due Process of Law Foundation*, vol. 5, no. 16 (June 2012), p. 5; and "Chipping at the Foundations: The Regional Justice System Comes Under Attack from the Countries Whose Citizens Need It Most," *Economist*, June 9, 2012.

[33] The human rights that the nations of the hemisphere have agreed to respect and guarantee are defined in the American Declaration of the Rights and Duties of Man, the American Convention on Human Rights, and the various other inter-American human rights treaties available at http://www.oas.org/en/iachr/mandate/basic_documents.asp.

[34] Ariel E. Dulitzky, "Twenty Reflections on the Process of Reflection," *Aportes: Magazine of the Due Process of Law Foundation*, vol. 5, no. 16 (June 2012), p. 11.

[35] Santiago Canton, "The Inter-American Commission on Human Rights: 50 Years of Advances and the New Challenges that Await," *Americas Quarterly*, (Summer 2009).

---

annually, and in 2013, it issued requests to governments in 22 cases.[36] Additionally, the IACHR observes the general human rights situations in member states, conducting on-site visits to carry out in-depth analyses; publishing special reports when warranted; and noting in its annual report which countries' human rights situations deserve special attention, follow-up, and monitoring. In its most recent annual report (issued in April 2014 and covering 2013), the IACHR made special note of the human rights situations in Cuba, Honduras, and Venezuela.[37] (For information on potential changes to the IACHR, see "Reform of the Inter-American Human Rights System" below).

Since 1990, the IACHR has created rapporteurships to draw attention to emerging human rights issues and certain groups that are particularly at risk of human rights violations due to vulnerability and discrimination. There are currently 10 rapporteurships, which focus on freedom of expression, human rights defenders, economic, social and cultural rights, and the rights of women, children, indigenous peoples, afro-descendants, prisoners, migrants, and lesbian, gay, trans, bisexual and intersex persons. These rapporteurships have been rather effective at drawing attention to potential abuses. In February 2012, for example, the Special Rapporteur for the Freedom of Expression immediately expressed deep concern after Ecuador's National Court of Justice affirmed criminal and civil judgments against three newspaper executives and a journalist that had been found guilty of "criminal defamation of an authority" for publishing a column critical of President Rafael Correa. The Rapporteur's vocal criticism helped initiate a wave of international outcry, which likely contributed to President Correa's decision not to enforce the sentences.[38]

The Inter-American Court of Human Rights, created in 1978, is an autonomous judicial institution charged with interpreting and applying the American Convention on Human Rights. Currently, 20 OAS member states accept the court's jurisdiction; the United States does not.[39] According to a number of analysts, the Inter-American Court has played an important role in the development of international human rights case law, securing justice for individual victims while facilitating structural changes to prevent future violations.[40]

The court, for example, has issued landmark rulings requiring states to investigate human rights violations and punish those responsible, regardless of any amnesty laws that they may have adopted. In February 2011, the court maintained this principle when ruling on the case of María Claudia García Iruretagoyena de Gelman. Ms. Gelman was an Argentine citizen who was detained by the Argentine military, transferred to Uruguay during the country's dictatorship, had her daughter taken from her shortly after giving birth, and then disappeared while in the custody of the Uruguayan security forces. In addition to awarding monetary damages to the daughter of Ms. Gelman, the court ordered Uruguay to carry out a full investigation of the case, and comply with its obligations under inter-American human rights treaties by ensuring that the country's

---

[36] Ibid; Inter-American Commission on Human Rights (IACHR), "Precautionary Measures," http://www.oas.org/en/iachr/decisions/precautionary.asp.

[37] IACHR, *Annual Report of the Inter-American Commission on Human Rights 2013*, April 23, 2014, http://www.oas.org/en/iachr/docs/annual/2013/TOC.asp.

[38] Special Rapporteurship for Freedom of Expression, "UN and IACHR Special Rapporteurs for Freedom of Expression State Deep Concern Over Decision to Affirm Judgment Against Journalists in Ecuador," Press Release, February 16, 2012; "Correa Pardons El Universo," *Latin News Daily Report*, February 28, 2012.

[39] Inter-American Court of Human Rights, *Annual Report 2013*, San José, Costa Rica, 2014, p.5, http://www.corteidh.or.cr/sitios/informes/docs/ENG/eng_2013.pdf.

[40] See, for example, Viviana Krsticevic, "The Promise of Protecting All," *Americas Quarterly*, (Summer 2009).

amnesty law is not an obstacle to investigating and punishing human rights violations.[41] In October 2011, the Uruguayan Congress passed legislation[42] to amend—and effectively overturn—the country's amnesty law, with proponents arguing that it was necessary in order to comply with the Inter-American Court of Human Rights' ruling.[43]

Economic and Social Development

Although the region has made considerable strides in terms of economic growth and social inclusion, poverty and inequality levels remain high in many countries, and the OAS continues to support development efforts. The organization's Department of Economic Development, Trade and Tourism, for example, supports efforts to enhance the productivity and competitiveness of economic actors in the region, with particular emphasis on micro, small, and medium-sized enterprises (MSMEs). It provides assistance to MSMEs designed to strengthen their capacities' to take advantage of trade and tourism opportunities, and encourages the use of science and technology to foster sustainable growth.[44]

The Special Multilateral Fund of the Inter-American Council for Integral Development (FEMCIDI) also supports development efforts. It was established in 1997 to address the most urgent needs of member states, especially those with smaller and more vulnerable economies. FEMCIDI projects are designed to strengthen institutions, build human capacity, and act as a seed fund for more far-reaching development programs. Current projects receiving FEMCIDI support are focused in the areas of culture, tourism, education, and science and technology. The fund also supports development efforts related to labor, the environment, social development, and economic diversification and trade liberalization.[45]

The Inter-American Social Protection Network is one of the more recent efforts by the OAS to foster economic and social development in the hemisphere. It was launched in September 2009 as a forum for member states to share experiences and best practices with regards to social protection systems. Over the past two decades, several countries in the region have implemented conditional cash transfer programs[46] or other innovative initiatives that have proven successful at reducing poverty and inequality. Through the Inter-American Social Protection Network, the OAS intends to facilitate the introduction of such programs to countries that have yet to establish effective social protection policies.[47]

---

[41] Inter-American Court of Human Rights, *Caso Gelman Vs. Uruguay: Sentencia*, February 24, 2011.

[42] In February 2013, Uruguay's Supreme Court ruled two articles of the legislation unconstitutional, effectively reinstituting the amnesty law.

[43] "Uruguay Overturns Amnesty for Military-era Crimes," *BBC News*, October 27, 2011.

[44] OAS, Executive Secretariat for Integral Development, Department of Economic Development, Trade and Tourism, *Promoting Economic Development in the Americas*, http://www.oas.org/en/sedi/dedtt/docs/brochure/progs_e.pdf.

[45] OAS, "FEMCIDI - Special Multilateral Fund of the Inter-American Council for Integral Development, Areas of Action" http://www.oas.org/en/sedi/femcidi/areas.asp.

[46] Conditional cash transfer programs, such as Mexico's *Oportunidades* and Brazil's *Bolsa Familia*, generally provide a cash stipend to poor families that commit to certain conditions, such as ensuring that their children are attending school and receiving preventative medical care. They are designed to provide short-term poverty alleviation while building human capital for long-term development.

[47] Hillary Rodham Clinton, Secretary of State, "Remarks at the Launch of the Inter-American Social Protection Network (IASPN)," U.S. Department of State, September 22, 2009; OAS, "OAS Assistant Secretary General Calls on Countries and International Organizations to Support the Inter-American Social Protection Network," Press Release, (continued...)

Regional Security Cooperation

In recent years, the OAS has dedicated greater attention to hemispheric security issues as member states have become increasingly concerned about transnational criminal threats. In 2005, the OAS created the Secretariat for Multidimensional Security in an attempt to address these security issues in a more comprehensive manner and better coordinate member states' efforts. The Secretariat supports a wide variety of activities, including efforts to reduce gang violence, prevent human trafficking, and remove land mines. Two issues that fall under the umbrella of regional security cooperation and may be of particular interest to Congress are illicit narcotics and terrorism.

Anti-drug Efforts

Concerns that the production, trafficking, and consumption of illegal narcotics posed a serious threat to the entire Western Hemisphere led OAS member states to establish the Inter-American Drug Abuse Control Commission (CICAD by its Spanish acronym) in 1986.[48] The commission's primary purpose is to develop and promote a comprehensive anti-drug policy for the region. CICAD's most recent hemispheric drug strategy was adopted in May 2010. It defines the world drug problem as "a complex, dynamic and multi-causal phenomenon" that requires "shared responsibility among all states."[49] The strategy includes over 50 guidelines for member states in the areas of institutional strengthening, demand reduction, supply reduction, control measures, and international cooperation. It also includes some policy shifts from the previous strategy, such as calling on member states to treat drug addiction as a public health matter and explore treatment and rehabilitation as alternatives to criminal prosecution.

In addition to formulating strategy, CICAD assists OAS member states in strengthening their anti-drug policies. It conducts research, develops and recommends legislation, and provides technical assistance and specialized training. CICAD also conducts assessments of member states' progress through its multilateral evaluation mechanism. Each member state is required to submit reports documenting their efforts to combat drug trafficking and related activities, which are then evaluated by a multidisciplinary group of experts who are appointed by each of the member states but do not evaluate their own countries. The experts identify strengths and weaknesses and offer recommendations.[50] For example, each of the five evaluations of the United States conducted since the 1999-2000 review period has noted that the country has yet to ratify the Inter-American Convention Against Illicit Manufacturing of and Trafficking in Firearms, Ammunition, Explosives and other Related Materials (CIFTA by its Spanish acronym), and has recommended that it do so.[51]

(...continued)

August 10, 2011.

[48] For more information on drug trafficking in the region, see CRS Report R41215, *Latin America and the Caribbean: Illicit Drug Trafficking and U.S. Counterdrug Programs,* coordinated by Clare Ribando Seelke.

[49] CICAD, *Hemispheric Drug Strategy,* May 2010, http://www.cicad.oas.org/Main/Template.asp?File=/main/aboutcicad/basicdocuments/strategy_2010_eng.asp.

[50] CICAD's country evaluations are available at http://www.cicad.oas.org/Main/Template.asp?File=/mem/reports/default_eng.asp.

[51] The Clinton Administration signed CIFTA in November 1997 and submitted the convention to the Senate, for its advice and consent, in June 1998 (Treaty Doc 105-49); the convention has never been acted upon. President Obama has called on the Senate to ratify CIFTA. The text of the treaty is available at http://foreign.senate.gov/download/?id=
(continued...)

Although some analysts contend that CICAD reinforces "Washington's hardline approach" to illicit narcotics,[52] others assert that the commission and its multilateral evaluation mechanism have been instrumental in building trust and establishing common ground for cooperation between the United States and other OAS member states.[53] After several regional leaders expressed frustration with the results of U.S.-backed counternarcotics policies, for example, the heads of state attending the Sixth Summit of the Americas called for the OAS to analyze the results of those policies and explore alternative approaches that may be more effective. In response, CICAD prepared two reports that were published in May 2013. Among other findings, the reports suggest that member states may benefit from greater policy flexibility, potentially including decriminalization of marijuana.[54] According to Secretary General Insulza, the reports are meant to inform the hemispheric debate and serve as a starting point for the region's leaders to establish collective and sustainable policies.[55] Member states will continue to discuss drug policy at a special session of the General Assembly scheduled to be held in Guatemala on September 19, 2014.

Anti-terrorism Efforts

In the aftermath of the 2001 terrorist attacks on the United States, the OAS took action to strengthen hemispheric cooperation against terrorism.[56] The OAS was the first international organization to formally condemn the attacks of September 11, adopting a Permanent Council resolution on September 19 that called the terrorist actions an "attack against all States of the Americas."[57] It also adopted a resolution, at Brazil's request, to invoke the Rio Treaty—the collective security pact of the Western Hemisphere.[58] A Meeting of Consultation of the Ministers of Foreign Affairs[59] adopted another resolution on September 21, which included provisions that called on OAS member states to "pursue, capture, prosecute, and punish ... the perpetrators, organizers, and sponsors" of the terrorist acts; deny terrorist groups the ability to operate within

---

(...continued)

E998994C-749B-4724-9AAA-82ACEB6A4850.

[52] Adam Isacson, "Conflict Resolution in the Americas: The Decline of the OAS," *World Politics Review*, May 22, 2012.

[53] Betty Horwitz, "The Role of the Inter-American Drug Abuse Control Commission (CICAD): Confronting the Problem of Illegal Drugs in the Americas," *Latin American Politics and Society*, vol. 52, no. 2 (Summer 2010).

[54] The reports, *The Drug Problem in the Americas* and *Scenarios for the Drug Problem in the Americas: 2013-2025*, are available at http://www.oas.org/documents/eng/press/Introduction_and_Analytical_Report.pdf and http://www.oas.org/documents/eng/press/Scenarios_Report.PDF.

[55] OAS Secretary General José Miguel Insulza, "Report on the Drug Problem in the Americas," Presentation at Chatham House, London, July 30, 2013.

[56] For more information on terrorism issues in the region, see CRS Report RS21049, *Latin America: Terrorism Issues*, by Mark P. Sullivan and June S. Beittel.

[57] OAS document, CP/RES. 796 (1293/01), *Convocation of the Twenty-Third Meeting of the Consultation of Ministers of Foreign Affairs*, September 19, 2011.

[58] OAS document, CP/RES. 797 (1293/01), *Convocation of the Twenty-Fourth Meeting of the Consultation of Ministers of Foreign Affairs to Serve as Organ of Consultation in Application of the Inter-American Treaty of Reciprocal Assistance*, September 19, 2011.

[59] According to Article 61 of the OAS Charter, a Meeting of Consultation of Ministers of Foreign Affairs may be called "in order to consider problems of an urgent nature and of common interest to the American States, and to serve as the Organ of Consultation." Article 65 of the Charter states that "in case of an armed attack on the territory of an American State or within the region of security delimited by the treaty in force, the Chairman of the Permanent Council shall without delay call a meeting of the Council to decide on the convocation of the Meeting of Consultation."

their territories; and strengthen anti-terrorism cooperation.[60] In June 2002, OAS member states adopted the Inter-American Convention Against Terrorism, through which they committed to take action against the financing of terrorism, ratify U.N. anti-terrorism instruments, improve cooperation among law enforcement, and deny asylum to suspected terrorists.[61]

Cooperation on terrorism issues has continued through the reinvigorated Inter-American Committee on Terrorism (CICTE by its Spanish acronym). CICTE was established in 1999 and serves as the primary forum for cooperation on terrorism issues within the hemisphere. It provides a range of programs to assist member states in preventing, combating, and eliminating terrorism, and meeting their commitments under the Inter-American Convention Against Terrorism. These programs support efforts in five areas: border controls, critical infrastructure protection, counter-terrorism legislative assistance, crisis management exercises, and promotion of international cooperation and partnerships.[62] In 2013, CICTE conducted 113 training courses, technical assistance missions, and other activities that benefited nearly 4,200 participants.[63]

Issues for Congress

Congress plays an important role in determining U.S. policy toward the OAS. As noted previously, the United States provided about 41% of the organization's funding in FY2013. Congress appropriates funds for the assessed contribution of the United States, as well as voluntary contributions to support specific projects in the hemisphere. Congress is also involved in the development of inter-American treaties, as any conventions negotiated by the executive branch must be submitted to the Senate for ratification. Moreover, Congress is charged with providing oversight of how U.S. funds are spent. Members of Congress frequently voice concerns over OAS actions (or lack thereof), and recommend changes in policy. Policy issues that have drawn particular interest from some Members of Congress in recent years include the potential reintegration of Cuba into the inter-American system, the application of the Inter-American Democratic Charter, efforts to reform the inter-American human rights system, the management and budget of the OAS, and the rise of alternative regional organizations.

---

[60] OAS document, RC.23/RES. 1/01, *Strengthening Hemispheric Cooperation to Prevent, Combat, and Eliminate Terrorism*, September 21, 2011.

[61] President Bush submitted the Inter-American Convention Against Terrorism to the Senate, for its advice and consent, in November 2002 (Treaty Doc. 107-18), and the Senate agreed to the resolution in October 2005. The text of the treaty is available at http://www.oas.org/juridico/english/treaties/a-66 html.

[62] James Patrick Kiernan, "Multidimensional Security in the Americas," *Americas*, vol. 63, no. 3 (May/June 2011).

[63] U.S. Department of State, Bureau of Counterterrorism, *Country Reports on Terrorism 2013*, April 2014, p. 248, http://www.state.gov/documents/organization/225886.pdf.

Reintegration of Cuba into the Inter-American System[64]

Background

Cuba was one of the founding members of the OAS, and as a signatory to the OAS Charter, remains a member of the organization. It has been excluded from participation since 1962, however, as a result of a decision at the Eighth Meeting of Consultation of the Ministers of Foreign Affairs to suspend Cuba for its adherence to Marxism-Leninism and alignment with the communist bloc.[65] The resolution to exclude Cuba was controversial at the time it was adopted, and the reintegration of Cuba into the inter-American system has remained a frequent source of contention among the countries of the hemisphere ever since.

At its June 2009 General Assembly, the OAS repealed the 1962 resolution that suspended Cuba from participation. In the lead up to the meeting, Secretary General Insulza and a number of member states asserted that the Cold War-era resolution was anachronistic and should be repealed.[66] While most member states agreed, there was considerable disagreement regarding when and how Cuba's eventual return to the OAS should take place. In the end, member states unanimously adopted a compromise measure that repealed the 1962 resolution, and stated that Cuba's participation in the OAS "will be the result of a process of dialogue initiated at the request of the Government of Cuba, and in accordance with the practices, purposes, and principles of the OAS,"[67] which include representative democracy and respect for human rights. Although the Cuban government declared the action a "major victory," it has stated that it has no interest in the OAS, and has made no effort to initiate a dialogue about its participation.[68]

Debate over Cuba's participation in the inter-American system was reignited in the lead up to the Sixth Summit of the Americas, which was held in Cartagena, Colombia in 2012. Although the summits traditionally have only included the participating members of the OAS, and the OAS serves as the technical secretariat for the summit process, the Summits of the Americas are not officially part of the OAS. The Cubans expressed interest in attending the Cartagena Summit after President Correa of Ecuador suggested that the countries of the Bolivarian Alliance (ALBA[69] by its Spanish acronym) would boycott if Cuba was not invited.[70] The Obama Administration opposed Cuba's inclusion in the Cartagena Summit,[71] and noted that the countries of the

---

[64] For more information on Cuba, its exclusion from the OAS, and U.S. policy toward the country, see CRS Report R40193, *Cuba: Issues for the 111th Congress*, and CRS Report R43024, *Cuba: U.S. Policy and Issues for the 113th Congress*, by Mark P. Sullivan.

[65] OAS document, Ser. C/II.8, *Eighth Meeting of Consultation of Ministers of Foreign Affairs*, January 22-31, 1962.

[66] Frances Robles, "OAS Chief Calls for Cuba's Reinstatement," *Miami Herald*, April 16, 2009.

[67] OAS document, AG/RES. 2438 (XXXIX-O/09), *Resolution on Cuba*, June 3, 2009.

[68] "Cuba Says No to OAS Membership," *Voice of America*, June 4, 2009; OAS, "Statement of the OAS Secretary General on the Summit of the Americas," Press Release, February 7, 2012; "Cuba Descarta Volver a OEA Pese a Invitar a Insulza a Cumbre de Celac," *Agence Frence Presse*, January 24, 2014.

[69] ALBA is a Venezuelan-led, socially oriented trade block. It includes Antigua and Barbuda, Bolivia, Cuba, Dominica, Ecuador, Nicaragua, Saint Lucia, Saint Vincent and the Grenadines, and Venezuela.

[70] "Cuba Quiere Estar en Cumbre de las Américas de Cartagena," *Agence France Presse*, February 6, 2012.

[71] Secretary of State Hillary Clinton, remarks during U.S. Congress, House Committee on Foreign Affairs, *Assessing U.S. Foreign Policy Priorities Amidst Economic Challenges: The Foreign Relations Budget for Fiscal Year 2013*, Hearing, 112th Cong., 2nd sess., February 29, 2012, Serial No. 112-132 (Washington: GPO, 2012), p. 11, http://foreignaffairs.house.gov/112/73119.pdf.

---

hemisphere declared at the 2001 Quebec Summit that "strict respect for the democratic system" is "an essential condition" for inclusion in the Summits of the Americas.[72] In an attempt to diffuse the situation, President Juan Manuel Santos of Colombia, the summit host, informed the Cubans that they would not be invited to Cartagena as a result of the lack of consensus, but that Cuba's future participation would be discussed.[73] At the summit, every country in the hemisphere—with the exceptions of Canada and the United States—reportedly voiced support for Cuba's inclusion at the next Summit of the Americas.[74] Panama, which is scheduled to host the Seventh Summit of the Americas in May 2015, reportedly intends to invite Cuba to participate.[75]

Policy Considerations

Since the early 1960s, U.S. policy toward Cuba has consisted largely of isolating the country through sanctions while providing support to the Cuban people. Although Members of Congress generally have agreed on the overall goals of U.S. policy—to help bring democracy and respect for human rights to the island—they have disagreed about how best to achieve those objectives. Some argue that maintaining strict sanctions is the only way to produce change in Cuba. Others argue that the United States is more likely to encourage reforms in the country by gradually increasing engagement or even swiftly normalizing relations.

Congressional debate surrounding the potential reintegration of Cuba into the inter-American system has largely reflected the disagreements over broader U.S. policy toward the island. Members of Congress who support efforts to isolate Cuba have opposed any attempt to reintegrate the country into the inter-American system. Some Members have called for the United States to boycott the Summit of the Americas if Cuba is allowed to participate.[76] They also introduced bills during the 112th Congress that would have prohibited U.S. contributions to the OAS if Cuba was allowed to participate in the organization or the Summits of the Americas before transitioning to democracy. Conversely, some Members who support greater U.S. engagement with Cuba have celebrated efforts that could pave the way to the country's inclusion in hemispheric institutions.[77]

Congressional actions related to Cuba's reintegration into the inter-American system could have broader implications for U.S. interests in the hemisphere. Congressional pressure designed to keep Cuba out of hemispheric institutions until it embraces democracy may continue to be successful given the desire of most countries in the region to maintain close relations with the United States and the OAS's reliance on consensus decision-making. However, such a policy also sets the United States against a nearly hemisphere-wide consensus to allow Cuban participation in

---

[72] *Declaration of Quebec City*, April 2001, http://www.summit-americas.org/iii_summit/iii_summit_dec_en.pdf.

[73] "Santos' Deft Diplomacy Saves Summit from Derailment," *Latin American Weekly Report*, March 8, 2012.

[74] Frank Bajak and Vivian Sequera, "US, Canada Alone at Summit in Cuba Stance," *Associated Press*, April 15, 2012.

[75] "Panamá Invitará a Cuba a la Cumbre de las Américas en 2015 (Canciller)," *Agence France Presse*, August 1, 2014.

[76] See, for example, Chairman Ileana Ros-Lehtinen, remarks during U.S. Congress, House Committee on Foreign Affairs, *Assessing U.S. Foreign Policy Priorities Amidst Economic Challenges: The Foreign Relations Budget for Fiscal Year 2013*, Hearing, 112th Cong., 2nd sess., February 29, 2012, Serial No. 112-132 (Washington: GPO, 2012), p.11, http://foreignaffairs house.gov/112/73119.pdf; and Representative David Rivera, remarks during U.S. Congress, House Committee on Foreign Affairs, Subcommittee on the Western Hemisphere, *Western Hemisphere Budget Review 2013: What Are U.S. Priorities?*, Hearing, 112th Cong., 2nd sess., April 25, 2012.

[77] See, for example, Office of Representative José Serrano, "Serrano Commends OAS Revocation of 1962 Anti-Cuba Resolution," Press Release, June 3, 2009.

the Summits of the Americas, and could continue to be a distraction at regional meetings and an obstacle to more cohesive hemispheric relations. Moreover, it could lead to a breakdown in the summit process. If Cuba is allowed to participate in the Summits of the Americas, the United States and the rest of the region could use the meetings to engage Cuba while still maintaining democracy and human rights as requirements for participation in the OAS itself. At the same time, by removing democratic governance as a precondition for participation in the summits, the nations of the hemisphere could send a signal that their commitment to democracy is less than absolute.

Application of the Inter-American Democratic Charter

Background

As noted previously, OAS member states adopted the Inter-American Democratic Charter in September 2001. The Democratic Charter begins by asserting that the peoples of the Americas have a right to democracy and their governments have an obligation to promote and defend it. It continues by noting that, in addition to free and fair elections, respect for human rights, the rule of law, political pluralism, and the separation of powers are all essential elements of representative democracy. The Democratic Charter calls on the OAS to promote democracy by carrying out electoral observation missions (when requested) and programs designed to promote democratic values and good governance. It also establishes mechanisms for collective action by member states when a nation's democratic institutions are under threat or have been overturned. The Democratic Charter states that "an unconstitutional interruption of the democratic order" in a member state is "an insurmountable obstacle to its government's participation" in the OAS, and allows the General Assembly to vote on suspension if diplomatic initiatives to restore democracy are unsuccessful.[78]

Since its adoption, there has been considerable debate within the hemisphere about how the provisions of the Inter-American Democratic Charter should be applied. While observers have called on member states to invoke the collective action mechanisms of the charter on numerous occasions, the OAS has done so in only a few cases. Analysts have identified three inter-related factors that have limited the operational scope of the Democratic Charter:

- tension between the principle of nonintervention enshrined in the OAS Charter[79] and the obligation to defend democracy through collective action;

- the lack of precise criteria for defining when a country has experienced a breakdown in the democratic order, and

- the inability of powers outside the executive branch to effectively access the OAS.[80]

---

[78] OAS, *Inter-American Democratic Charter*, http://www.oas.org/OASpage/eng/Documents/Democractic_Charter.htm.

[79] Article 19 of the OAS Charter states, "No State or group of States has the right to intervene, directly or indirectly, for any reason whatever, in the internal or external affairs of any other State. The foregoing principle prohibits not only armed force but also any other form of interference or attempted threat against the personality of the State or against its political, economic, and cultural elements."

[80] OAS document, CJI/RES. 160 (LXXV-O/09), *Follow-up on the Application of the Inter-American Democratic Charter*, August 12, 2009, p. 23.

Although OAS member states accepted that democratic breakdowns justify collective action when they adopted the Democratic Charter, they also placed limits on the charter's application in order to defend the principle of nonintervention. The OAS is not allowed to intervene in situations where democratic institutions appear to be threatened unless the country requests assistance and collective action without a member state's consent can only take place after a rupture in the democratic order has already taken place.[81] In Honduras, for example, polarization between governmental institutions had been building for several months before then President Manuel Zelaya was arrested by the military and forced into exile in June 2009. The Honduran government did not request OAS assistance until shortly before the ouster, however, and Zelaya was removed from office a day before an OAS special commission was due to arrive in the country to assess the situation and attempt to resolve the conflict through dialogue.[82] Consequently, the member states were unable to take collective action in Honduras until the country was already in crisis. The unanimous decision to suspend[83] Honduras from the OAS and subsequent diplomatic efforts were incapable of reversing the situation.[84]

The Democratic Charter's failure to define what constitutes "an unconstitutional interruption of the democratic order" has further limited its application. In several countries in the region, democratically elected leaders have engaged in actions that generally follow constitutional procedures but eliminate checks and balances considered by many analysts to be integral to representative democracy. Since the Democratic Charter is not clear about whether such actions are violations, member states have been unwilling to respond, deferring instead to the principle of nonintervention. In December 2010, for example, the outgoing Venezuelan Congress granted then President Hugo Chávez the power to legislate by decree for 18 months. Although the stated purpose of the so-called "enabling law" was to speed recovery efforts after destructive storms in 2010, President Chávez used the law to approve over 50 measures ranging from rewriting the labor code to nationalizing the gold industry.[85] Secretary General Insulza and other observers asserted that the law violated the spirit and letter of the Democratic Charter,[86] however, member states chose not to invoke it.[87]

The composition of the OAS has served as a third barrier to applying the Democratic Charter. The members of the Permanent Council, who are charged with assessing democratic crises under the charter, represent their nations' executive branches. Accordingly, they have interpreted the Democratic Charter's requirement that the OAS receive consent from "the government concerned" prior to intervention to mean consent from the nation's executive power. As a result, other branches of government and civil society groups are effectively unable to invoke the charter's collective action mechanisms. In Ecuador, for example, then President Lucio Gutierrez

---

[81] See Chapter IV of the Democratic Charter, "Strengthening and Preservation of Democratic Institutions."

[82] OAS, "Engagement in Honduras, November 2008-July 2009," July 2009.

[83] Honduras was the first member state to be suspended under the Inter-American Democratic Charter. OAS member states did not lift the suspension until June 1, 2011, after an election had taken place and the Honduran government had dropped criminal charges against Zelaya and allowed him to return to the country.

[84] For more information on the political crisis in Honduras, see CRS Report R41064, *Honduran Political Crisis, June 2009-January 2010*, and CRS Report RL34027, *Honduras: Background and U.S. Relations*, by Peter J. Meyer.

[85] Ezequiel Minaya, "Chavez's Decree Powers Expire, but Not Before Heavy Use," *Dow Jones International News*, June 18, 2012.

[86] "Faced with the Democratic Charter, Chávez Beats a Hasty Retreat," *Latin American Security & Strategic Review*, January 2011.

[87] For more information on democracy in Venezuela, see CRS Report R43239, *Venezuela: Background and U.S. Relations*, by Mark P. Sullivan.

dissolved the Supreme Court of Justice in December 2004. Although some within the country called for the Democratic Charter to be invoked, OAS member states took no action. It was only in April 2005, after the Ecuadoran Congress had removed Gutiérrez and the new President, Alfredo Palacio, requested OAS assistance, that member states sent a mission to the country.[88]

Policy Considerations

Democracy promotion has long been a goal of U.S. policy toward Latin America and the Caribbean. Congress has supported successive administrations' efforts, appropriating foreign assistance designed to strengthen democratic governance and institutions as well as civil society in order to hold governments accountable. In recent years, Members of Congress have lauded the significant advances that have occurred in most of the hemisphere while raising concerns about the declining quality of democracy in a few nations.[89]

The role of the OAS in promoting democracy is more contested. Some Members assert that "the OAS continues to fail to live up to its obligations to support the respect for human rights and uphold democratic principles."[90] They maintain that recent elections in countries such as Venezuela and Nicaragua were illegitimate, and that the OAS has failed to meet its obligations given its lack of action. Among other reforms to the organization, they have called for a broader application of the Democratic Charter. A provision of the Venezuelan Human Rights and Democracy Protection Act (H.R. 4587, Ros-Lehtinen), passed by the House in May 2014, would direct the U.S. Permanent Representative to the OAS to "use the voice, vote, and influence of the United States...to defend and protect the Inter-American Democratic Charter."

Other Members of Congress have argued that, despite its flaws, the OAS is "the best thing we have to ensure democracy in the Western Hemisphere."[91] They maintain that the organization's electoral observation missions and human rights bodies continue to carry out crucial work that strengthens democracy in member states, and that the United States should coordinate more closely with allies in the region to improve the organization. They have also noted that democracy activists in some countries have called for continued U.S. support for the OAS. In 2011, for example, members of the Venezuelan political opposition reportedly asserted that cutting U.S. funding for the OAS would "jeopardize the opportunity to restore democracy and the rule of law" in their nation.[92]

Although there is agreement among many Members of Congress that the OAS should apply the Democratic Charter more broadly, there appears to be little appetite in the region—even among U.S. allies—for such actions. Given the asymmetrical power relations and the long history of U.S. intervention in the hemisphere, many nations are wary of establishing precedents for foreign

---

[88] OAS document, CP/doc. 4184/07, *The Inter-American Democratic Charter*, April 4, 2007, p. 14.

[89] See, for example, U.S. Congress, House Committee on Foreign Affairs, Subcommittee on the Western Hemisphere, *Challenges to Democracy in the Western Hemisphere*, Hearing, 113th Cong., 1st sess., September 10, 2013.

[90] See, for example, Office of Representative Ileana Ros-Lehtinen, "The OAS Fails to Live Up to Its Inter-American Democratic Charter and Reforms are Desperately Needed to Protect American Taxpayers, Says Ros-Lehtinen," Press Release, July 24, 2013.

[91] Representative Eliot Engel, remarks during U.S. Congress, House Committee on Foreign Affairs, Subcommittee on the Western Hemisphere, *Markup on H.R. 3401 and H.R. 2542*, Hearing, 112th Cong., 1st sess., December 15, 2011, Serial No. 112-115 (Washington: GPO, 2011).

[92] Mary Beth Sheridan, "Venezuelan Opposition Resists Republican Measure," *Washington Post*, August 6, 2011.

involvement in internal affairs.[93] Indeed, they have often used the OAS to engage in defensive multilateralism designed to constrain unilateral U.S. action.[94] Given this aversion to intervention, member states are unlikely to invoke the collective action mechanisms of the Democratic Charter in the near term except in cases of democratic breakdowns that resemble traditional coups d'état.

Reform of the Inter-American Human Rights System

Background

Despite the inter-American human rights system's reputation as one of the most effective parts of the OAS, member states have regularly recommended changes to the hemisphere's human rights bodies. A 2008-2009 review of the IACHR, for example, led the commission to adopt new rules of procedure related to granting precautionary measures, processing petitions of alleged human rights violations, referring cases to the Inter-American Court, and holding public hearings on human rights conditions in member states. In June 2011, just a year and a half after the IACHR's new rules of procedure went into effect, the OAS Permanent Council initiated another evaluation of the commission by creating the "Special Working Group to Reflect on the Workings of the Inter-American Commission on Human Rights with a View to Strengthening the Inter-American System for the Protection of Human Rights."[95]

Although the special working group was ostensibly established to strengthen the inter-American human rights system, some civil society groups feared it would do the opposite.[96] The impetus for the working group's creation—Brazil's negative reaction to an IACHR precautionary measure request[97]—suggested that the review might be more focused on constraining the actions of the commission than supporting it. Some OAS member states' presentations to the special working group reinforced this perception. They included calls to adopt more stringent criteria for granting precautionary measures, shift the focus of the IACHR's work away from individual cases toward general human rights promotion, remove the independent budget and staff of the Special Rapporteur for Freedom of Expression, and end the practice of identifying countries that have human rights situations that deserve special attention in the IACHR's annual report.[98]

The special working group issued a report in December 2011 that provoked a mixed reaction in the hemisphere. While civil society groups welcomed some aspects of the report, they asserted

---

[93] OAS document, CJI/RES. 160 (LXXV-O/09), *Follow-up on the Application of the Inter-American Democratic Charter*, August 12, 2009, p. 27.

[94] Thomas Legler, "Multilateralism and Regional Governance in the Americas," in *Latin American Multilateralism: New Directions* (Ottawa: FOCAL, 2010), p. 13.

[95] IACHR, *Position Document on the Process of Strengthening of the Inter-American System for the Protection of Human Rights*, April 8, 2012, http://www.oas.org/en/iachr/docs/pdf/PosicionFortalecimientoENG.pdf.

[96] Diego Urdaneta, "OEA Aprueba Mejoras para la CIDH, pero ONG Denuncian Intento de Erosionarla," *Agence France Presse*, January 25, 2012.

[97] In April 2011, the IACHR issued a precautionary measure that ordered Brazil to halt construction on a hydroelectric dam in order to protect indigenous communities. Brazil denounced the measure as "unjustifiable," withdrew its Ambassador to the OAS, and withheld its assessed contribution. Ministério das Relações Exteriores, "Solicitação da Comissão Interamericana de Direitos Humanos (CIDH) da OEA," Nota à Imprensa N° 142, April 5, 2011; Amato, June 2012, op. cit., p. 5.

[98] OAS document, GT/SIDH-17/11 rev.1, *Compilation of Presentations by Member States on the Topics of the Working Group*, November 7, 2011.

---

that other portions "could trigger a process of weakening the inter-American human rights system."[99] The report recognized that autonomy and independence are essential for the IACHR to carry out its mission, recommended that member states adopt the inter-American human rights treaties to assure the universality of the system, and called on the OAS to gradually increase the resources allocated to the human rights bodies. At the same time, the report included some member state suggestions that human rights defenders viewed as problematic. For example, it recommended that the IACHR broaden (and thereby potentially weaken) the chapter of its report that currently identifies the countries experiencing the greatest difficulties in protecting human rights by including every country in the region and considering economic, social, and cultural rights in addition to civil and political rights.[100]

Despite these concerns, the 2012 OAS General Assembly approved a resolution that welcomed the special working group's report, and instructed the Permanent Council to draw up proposals for its application to be presented to a special session of the General Assembly. The United States attached a footnote to the resolution that indicated it would not block consensus, but asserted that no efforts should be undertaken to force the implementation of the nonbinding recommendations.[101] The IACHR effectively vetoed the reform recommendations that human rights groups had viewed as most problematic by adopting a series of relatively minor changes to its rules of procedure, policies, and practices on March 19, 2013.[102] Although countries such as Bolivia, Ecuador, and Venezuela tried to override the IACHR's decisions and push through more radical changes at a special session of the General Assembly on March 22, 2013, the vast majority of OAS member states rejected the attempt. Subsequent efforts to push through extensive changes to the IACHR have also been rejected.[103]

Policy Considerations

Members of Congress frequently have expressed support for the inter-American human rights system. In the report (S.Rept. 113-195) accompanying the FY2015 Department of State, Foreign Operations, and Related Programs Appropriations Act (S. 2499), for example, the Senate Appropriations Committee recognizes "the essential role of the IACHR in providing justice for victims of human rights violations and protecting fundamental freedoms in many Latin American countries whose justice systems are weak and influenced by corruption." The bill would also provide $2 million for the IACHR, including $500,000 for the Special Rapporteur for Freedom of Expression. In addition, several Members spoke out against attempts to weaken the IACHR in the lead up the March 2013 special session of the General Assembly,[104] and a bill introduced in April

---

[99] Instituto de Defensa Legal; Centro de Estudios Legales y Sociales; Due Process of Law Foundation; Centro de Estudios de Derecho, Justicia y Sociedad; Conectas Direitos Humanos; Fundación Construir, *Position of Civil Society Organizations of the Americas on the Final Report of the Special Working Group to Reflect on the Workings of the Inter-American Commission on Human Rights with a view to Strengthening the Inter-American Human Rights System*, January 21, 2012.

[100] Ibid; OAS document, AG/doc. 5310/12 *Report of the Special Working Group to Reflect on the Workings of the Inter-American Commission on Human Rights With a View to Strengthening the Inter-American Human Rights System for Consideration by the Permanent Council*, May 26, 2012.

[101] OAS document, AG/RES. 2761 (XLII-O/12) *Follow-Up on the Recommendations Contained in the "Report of the Special Working Group to Reflect on the Workings of the Inter-American Commission on Human Rights with a View to Strengthening the Human Rights System,"* June 5, 2012.

[102] IACHR, Resolution 1/2013, *Reform of the Rules of Procedure, Policies, and Practices*, March 19, 2013.

[103] "Insulza Ringfences the OAS, for Now," *Laitn News Daily Report*, June 6, 2014.

[104] See, for example, Representative Eliot L. Engel, "Strengthening the Inter-American Human Rights System," *The* (continued...)

2013 (H.R. 1687, Ros-Lehtinen) includes a provision that would direct the U.S. Permanent Representative to the OAS to "use the voice, vote, and influence of the United States" to "defend, protect, and strengthen" the IACHR.

Despite these demonstrations of support for the IACHR, some analysts argue that the United States lacks credibility in defending the human rights body given its unwillingness to ratify the hemisphere's human rights treaties.[105] The United States has signed only one such treaty, the American Convention on Human Rights, which created the Inter-American Court and defines the human rights that countries of the hemisphere agree to respect as well as many of the functions and procedures of the IACHR. Although the Carter Administration submitted the treaty to the Senate for its advice and consent in 1978 (Treaty Doc. 95-21),[106] the Senate has never acted on it. Moreover, while the United States is currently subject to the jurisdiction of the IACHR under the American Declaration of the Rights and Duties of Man (adopted in 1948 alongside the OAS Charter), the U.S. government argues that the declaration does not create legally binding obligations and thus cannot be violated.[107] This has contributed to the creation of a multi-tiered[108] human rights system in the hemisphere that many OAS member states view as problematic.

Given these criticisms, some analysts argue that the United States could better assert leadership on human rights issues in the hemisphere by ratifying the various inter-American human rights treaties. While subjecting the United States to the same legally binding obligations that the majority of the nations of the hemisphere already accept would likely increase U.S. credibility on the issue, some policy makers have raised concerns about potential conflicts with U.S. law and international interference in U.S. domestic affairs.[109] Alternatively, some observers contend that the U.S. government could demonstrate greater support for the inter-American human rights system by doing more to act on the IACHR's criticisms of various U.S. policies and its recommendations for improving human rights in the United States. While the resources the United States provides are necessary for the IACHR to carry out its duties, the United States will likely continue to face criticism from some in the hemisphere that such donations allow the United States to promote its interests without assuming any obligations.[110]

(...continued)

Hill, March 22, 2013; and Senator Patrick Leahy, "Free Speech in the Americas," remarks in the Senate, *Congressional Record*, vol. 159, issue 41 (March 20, 2013), p. S2020.

[105] See, for example, "Human Rights in the Americas: Chipping at the Foundations," *The Economist*, June 9, 2012; "Global Insider: Inter-American Commission Reforms Seek to Change a Mixed System," *World Politics Review*, March 11, 2013; and Mari Hayman, "ALBA-Backed Proposals for IACHR Reform Could Undermine the System," *World Politics Review*, March 27, 2013.

[106] The text of the treaty, as received in the Senate, is available at http://www.foreign.senate.gov/download/?id= C0C737E4-51E1-407B-8449-761FF02BE220.

[107] See, for example, Inter-American Commission on Human Rights, "Response of the Government of the United States of America to Inter-American Commission on Human Rights Report 85/100 of October 23, 2000 Concerning Mariel Cubans (Case 9903)," http://www.cidh.org/Respuestas/USA.9903 htm.

[108] Currently, 20 nations accept the jurisdiction of the Inter-American Court and the full jurisdiction of the IACHR under the American Convention, three other nations do not accept the jurisdiction of the court but have ratified the American Convention, and 12 nations—including the United States—have not ratified (or have withdrawn from) the American Convention and are only subject to the jurisdiction of the IACHR under the American Declaration.

[109] For a variety of views, concerns, and recommendations regarding the American Convention on Human Rights, see U.S. Congress, Senate Committee on Foreign Relations, *International Human Rights Treaties*, Hearings, 96th Cong., 1st sess., November 14, 15, 16, and 19, 1979 (Washington: GPO, 1980).

[110] "Global Insider: Inter-American Commission Reforms Seek to Change a Mixed System," *World Politics Review*, March 11, 2013.

Management and Budget Concerns

Background

The OAS has faced persistent budget shortfalls for a number of years. Member states' contributions to the Regular Fund have remained relatively stagnant for much of the past two decades as a result of their reluctance to adjust country quotas. At the same time, member states have required the OAS to provide annual cost of living increases to its employees, and have given the organization an increasing number of mandates. A recent review found that the OAS has more than 750 mandates addressing nearly every issue facing the nations of the hemisphere.[111] This combination of frozen funding levels and increasing costs and responsibilities created a structural deficit at the OAS.

After taking office in 2005, Secretary General Insulza repeatedly warned that the OAS would be forced to make serious cuts if member states remained unwilling to increase their assessed contributions. While OAS member states approved a few minor quota adjustments, annual expenditures continued to exceed revenues and the OAS had to use resources from its reserve fund and member state payments of back dues to bridge the gap. These financial reserves were exhausted by 2010. The OAS has ended each of the fiscal years since then with a budget deficit. To find savings, the OAS has deferred required infrastructure costs and information technology upgrades. It has also lost a quarter of its staff over the past five years.[112]

Despite deferring costs and reducing personnel, the organization's financial situation remains precarious. As of December 31, 2013, the OAS had a deficit of $663,000.[113] Since the organization has exhausted its reserve fund, even temporary delays in receiving expected revenues can lead to cash shortfalls. In 2011, for example, the OAS was forced to borrow from its Scholarship and Training Program Fund in order to sustain daily operations after Brazil withheld its contributions over a disagreement with the IACHR.[114] Moreover, the organization reportedly faces costs of nearly $16 million for the repair and updating of its property.[115]

According to OAS officials and many outside analysts, the organization's recurring budgetary problems are "a demoralizing institutional weakness" that constrains the organization's ability to plan ahead, recruit and retain top level staff, and establish priorities.[116] The unwillingness of member states to increase contributions to the Regular Fund has made the OAS more reliant on voluntary funds that vary from year to year. OAS officials maintain that this change has made it more difficult for the organization to make medium- and long-term plans. They also maintain that this uncertainty makes it difficult to recruit staff and keep more qualified personnel, which in turn has weakened the organization's institutional identity.[117]

---

[111] OAS document, CP/CAAP -3308/14, *Results of the Mandate Classification Exercise*, July 14, 2014.

[112] OAS document, JAE/doc. 44/14, 2013 *Report to the Permanent Council: Annual Audit of Accounts and Financial Statements for the Years Ended December 31, 2013 and 2012*, April 30, 2014, p.3.

[113] Ibid.

[114] "SOS por la OEA," *Semana* (Colombia), March 24, 2012.

[115] OAS document, JAE/doc. 44/14, 2013 *Report to the Permanent Council: Annual Audit of Accounts and Financial Statements for the Years Ended December 31, 2013 and 2012*, April 30, 2014, p.9.

[116] Inter-American Dialogue, June 2006, op. cit. p. 8.

[117] OAS document, CP/INF. 6248/11, *Proposal for Financing the 2012 Program-Budget of the Organization of* (continued...)

Policy Considerations

Members of the 113th Congress have expressed concerns about the management and budget of the OAS, and have adopted legislation designed to strengthen the organization. On October 2, 2013, President Obama signed into law the OAS Revitalization and Reform Act of 2013 (P.L. 113-41), which had been passed by both houses of Congress in September 2013. Among other provisions, the measure calls on the OAS to implement a results-based budgeting process to prioritize its core functions and reduce its mandates, implement transparent and merit-based human resource processes, and alter its fee structure so that within five years no member state pays more than 50% of the organization's assessed dues.[118] The legislation directed the Secretary of State to develop a strategy for ensuring that the OAS adopts these reforms and to provide quarterly briefings to Congress on their implementation.

Many of the reforms supported by Congress echo previous suggestions by Secretary General Insulza and several of them are already in the process of being implemented. In his December 2011 presentation, "A Strategic Vision of the OAS," Insulza called for the organization to allocate Regular Fund resources exclusively to core functions, adopt a human resources policy that institutionalizes a merit-based career service, and introduce a rule to ensure that no member state pays more than 49% of the organization's assessed dues.[119] The OAS has established a Working Group on the Review of OAS Programs, which has reportedly made considerable progress in reviewing and prioritizing OAS mandates and drafting changes to the organization's human resources policy.[120]

The 2014 General Assembly adopted a resolution on "Progress toward Accountability, Efficiency and Effectiveness, and Results in the OAS General Secretariat." The resolution instructs the Permanent Council to establish a methodology for prioritizing OAS mandates and to begin implementing it. The resolution also authorizes the Permanent Council to approve amendments to the organization's human resource policies. Other provisions of the resolution instruct the General Secretariat to continue efforts toward the adoption of International Public Sector Accounting Standards (IPSAS), realign the organization's resources and structure with its mandates, and present a Strategic Plan for Management Modernization that includes proposals for simplifying operations, creating efficiencies, and avoiding waste and duplicated efforts.[121]

Despite these efforts, some Members of Congress continue to express concerns about the management and budget of the OAS. The report (S.Rept. 113-195) accompanying the FY2015 Department of State, Foreign Operations, and Related Programs Appropriations Act (S. 2499), for example, states that the Senate Appropriations Committee "remains concerned that OAS personnel practices are not sufficiently transparent or merit based and that in a time of severe budget constraints the OAS has not done enough to eliminate unnecessary costs."

(...continued)

American States, May 13, 2011.

[118] OAS, Office of the Secretary General, *Proposed Program-Budget, 2014*, August 5, 2013.

[119] OAS document, CP/doc.4673/11, *Note of the Secretary General to the Chair of the Permanent Council Presenting "A Strategic Vision of the OAS,"* December 19, 2011.

[120] OAS document, CAAP/GT/RVPP-203/13, *Methodology and Work Plan for the Working Group on the Review of OAS Programs (September 2013-May 2014)*, August 27, 2013.

[121] OAS document, AG/RES. 2815 (XLIV-O/14), *Progress Towards Accountability, Efficiency and Effectiveness, and Results in the OAS General Secretariat*, June 4, 2014.

Regional Alternatives to the OAS

Background

Over the years, countries in the Western Hemisphere have formed a number of regional organizations designed to promote economic integration and political cooperation. These include blocs originally created to advance trade relations such as the Caribbean Community (CARICOM), the Common Market of the South (Mercosur by its Spanish acronym), and the Pacific Alliance, as well as organizations with more political orientations such as the leftist Bolivarian Alliance (ALBA by its Spanish acronym), the Union of South American Nations (UNASUR by its Spanish acronym), and the Community of Latin American and Caribbean States (CELAC by its Spanish acronym). While these groups vary in size, purpose, and effectiveness, none of them include the United States or Canada.

As countries of the hemisphere have become more independent and regional organizations have proliferated, a number of governments have suggested that the newer organizations should take on some of the roles that have traditionally been played by the OAS. Some leaders in the region assert that the OAS is dominated by the United States, and is little more than a tool for U.S. foreign policy. Consequently, they argue that the nations of the hemisphere would be better served by replacing the OAS with CELAC, which includes all of Latin America and the Caribbean but excludes the United States and Canada.[122] Others in the region are opposed to replacing the OAS, but have suggested that the smaller regional blocs may be able to complement the organization's work. Moreover, they argue that these organizations may be more effective than the OAS in certain cases, such as mediating disputes within their sub-regions.[123] UNASUR, for example, helped resolve internal political conflicts in Bolivia in 2008 and Ecuador in 2010.[124]

While many analysts acknowledge that the newer regional organizations can play important roles in the hemisphere, they also note that these groups have their own flaws. There is considerable variation among the regional organizations; however, most lack strong, independent, and well-financed secretariats capable of receiving mandates and carrying out programs.[125] Instead, they often rely on high-level diplomacy and presidential summits, which can be useful for promoting political dialogue, but rarely result in significant, ongoing initiatives. Given these limitations, a number of analysts maintain that the OAS remains the pre-eminent political institution of the hemisphere. An Inter-American Dialogue task force on the OAS, for example, asserted that "no other organization has the necessary credibility and mandate to bring together the collective influence of the hemisphere's countries to resolve disputes among member states, encourage compromise among governments on salient regional issues, credibly monitor national

---

[122] "The Caracas Consensus," *Latin News Daily Report*, December 2, 2011; Maye Primera, "Chávez Fracasa en el Intento de que Latinoamérica Prescinda de la OEA," *El País* (Argentina), December 3, 2011.

[123] "La OEA y la CELAC Son Complementarias, Afirma Canciller de Costa Rica," *Agence France Presse*, January 21, 2014; "Mercosur y UNASUR Pueden Ser 'Más Efectivos' que la OEA (Amorim)," *Agence France Presse*, September 11, 2010.

[124] "Latin America Goes It Alone as Bolivian Conflict Explodes," *Latin American Weekly Report*, September 18, 2008; "Resolution of Ecuadorean Crisis is a Victory for UNASUR," *Latin American Regional Report: Brazil & Southern Cone*, October 2010.

[125] Thomas Legler and Lesley Burns, "Introduction," in *Latin American Multilateralism: New Directions* (Ottawa: FOCAL, 2010), p. 6.

government performance on sensitive concerns, and press countries to change when they violate hemispheric norms."[126]

Policy Considerations

The rise of regional alternatives to the OAS presents both potential opportunities and challenges for the United States. One potential benefit of such organizations might be an increase in burden-sharing in the hemisphere. As the newer organizations evolve, they may be able to take on more responsibility for maintaining peace and stability in their sub-regions, which could enable Congress to dedicate scarce U.S. resources to other priorities. A division of labor among various organizations might also enable the OAS to better concentrate its efforts on its core agenda and thereby carry out its mandates more effectively.

At the same time, an increasing role for other multilateral organizations could lead to a weaker, more divided OAS. If other organizations take on larger roles in the hemisphere, the role of the OAS would likely decline. Some Members of Congress argue that such a development could weaken U.S. influence in the region since the OAS is one of the few multilateral organizations in the hemisphere in which the United States is a member and shapes policy decisions.[127] Moreover, the proliferation of regional organizations could further weaken the hemisphere's ability to speak with one voice. For example, Mercosur and Unasur determined that the rapid June 2012 impeachment of Paraguayan President Fernando Lugo constituted a break in the democratic order and sought to isolate the country by suspending it from participation.[128] The OAS, on the other hand, concluded that the impeachment did not constitute a coup d'état, and member states decided not to suspend Paraguay from participating in the organization.[129] Similarly, UNASUR electoral observation missions adhere to less rigorous standards than those of the OAS, potentially legitimizing flawed elections.[130]

The impetus behind the creation of some of the new regional organizations also has implications for the United States. Latin American leaders have established new multilateral institutions for a number of reasons, one of which is the lingering view of many in the region that the OAS is an institution dominated by the United States. Even as some Members of Congress assert that the organization acts against U.S. interests, a number of policy makers in the broader region argue that the OAS imposes U.S. policies. Given these views, some analysts maintain that "any reform to the OAS that begins in Washington, especially in the U.S. Congress, can have the potential to backfire" and provoke opposition in the hemisphere.[131]

---

[126] Inter-American Dialogue, June 2006, op. cit., p. 6.

[127] See, for example, Representative Gregory W. Meeks, "Organization of American States Revitalization and Reform Act of 2013," Remarks in the House, *Congressional Record*, vol. 159, part 122 (September 17, 2013), pp. H5567-H5569.

[128] "Brazil Calls OAS to Consider Mercosur and Unasur Statements on Paraguay," *MercoPress*, July 13, 2012.

[129] OAS, "Report by the Mission of the OAS Secretary General and Delegation to the Republic of Paraguay – Non Official Version," Press Release, July 10, 2012; "OAS Will Not Sanction Paraguay, Says Ambassador Following Informal Meeting," *MercoPress*, July 23, 2012.

[130] Christopher Sabatini, "Meaningless Multilateralism: In International Diplomacy, South America Chooses Quantity Over Quality," *Foreign Affairs*, August 8, 2014.

[131] Mauricio Cárdenas, remarks during *Latin America's New Political Landscape and the Future of the Organization of American States*, Brookings Institution, Washington, DC, March 15, 2010.

Outlook

In 1948, Alberto Lleras Camargo, the first Secretary General of the OAS, asserted "the organization ... is what the member governments want it to be and nothing else."[132] This has held true throughout the organization's history with the OAS engaging in activities and adopting new areas of focus in accordance with the decisions of member states. As an organization composed of 35 diverse nations that operates based on consensus, however, the OAS is often slow to arrive at decisions and prone to inaction. This is especially the case when the hemisphere is ideologically polarized or addressing contentious topics. Nevertheless, even when member states are incapable of establishing consensus on a given issue, the OAS continues to carry out a variety of activities to advance the organization's broad objectives: democracy promotion, human rights protection, economic and social development, and regional security cooperation.

As the organization's largest financial contributor and the hemisphere's most powerful nation, the United States remains influential within the OAS. The organization's objectives in the region are largely consistent with those of the United States, and many of its activities complement U.S. efforts. At the same time, OAS actions (or the lack thereof) do not always align with the organization's stated objectives, and the United States' ability to advance its policy initiatives in the organization has declined over the past decade. These conflicting tendencies are likely to continue in the coming years, spurring on the congressional debate over the utility of the OAS for advancing U.S. interests in the Western Hemisphere.

Author Contact Information

Peter J. Meyer
Analyst in Latin American Affairs
pmeyer@crs.loc.gov, 7-5474

---

[132] *U.S.-Latin American Policymaking: A Reference Handbook*, ed. David W. Dent (Westport, CT: Greenwood Press, 1995), p. 27.